AF234511

POCKET IMAGES

Wingham, Adisham & Littlebourne

POCKET IMAGES

Wingham, Adisham & Littlebourne

Maurice A. Crane

NONSUCH

First published 1993
This new pocket edition 2007
Images unchanged from first edition

Nonsuch Publishing Limited
Cirencester Road, Chalford
Stroud, Gloucestershire, GL6 8PE
www.nonsuch-publishing.com

Nonsuch Publishing is an imprint of NPI Media Group

© Maurice A. Crane, 1993

The right of Maurice A. Crane to be identified as the Author
of this work has been asserted in accordance with the
Copyrights, Designs and Patents Act 1988.

British Library Cataloguing in Publication Data.
A catalogue record for this book is available from the British Library.

ISBN 978-1-84588-435-2

Typesetting and origination by NPI Media Group
Printed in Great Britain

Contents

Wingham Well windmill, 1908. The last miller to work it was Mr Maplesden in the last decade of the nineteenth century. Much of the tower mill was demolished in 1964, leaving only the ground floor as a fruit store.

One

Wingham

Wingham's origins can be traced back more than 1,700 years to when the Romans settled by the crossing of the river, the position on the main route to Canterbury from the Roman port of Rutupiae (Richborough) making it an ideal site for a Roman villa, part of which was excavated in 1881.

Later, the Anglo-Saxon Jutes, who followed the Romans, probably gave Wingham its name. 'Wigga' in Old English means fighter or warrior, and 'ham' the homestead or hamlet belonging to him and his people. Shortly after St Augustine brought Christianity to Kent in 597, a place of worship, probably a wooden structure, was erected on the site of today's church. Nothing remains of this building, and the earliest parts of the present structure date from its rebuilding in Norman times.

We do know that the village owes its early size and importance to its situation. Sited along the route from London to Europe via Canterbury and the main port of Sandwich, it would have been an ideal place for kings and other royal travellers to have halted on their way to and from France. It became the main legal and judicial centre in the area and also, when King Edmund gave the manor of Wingham to the Archbishop of Canterbury in 941, the key ecclesiastical centre. By the eleventh century, according to the survey made by the monks of Christ Church, Canterbury, the 'Domesday Monachorum', it had become the largest of the archbishop's personal landholdings.

By the thirteenth century, Wingham had become large enough to cause the archbishop to make plans for expansion into a new town. Side turnings were laid out off its main street, where large numbers of timber-framed houses were constructed. The weekly market, a lucrative enterprise that was held every Tuesday, acquired a market house. Numerous inns grew up to serve the increased traffic, among them the Red Lion which is still standing today.

In order to better administer Wingham's increasingly important pastoral and ecclesiastical role, a college of secular canons was established. This resulted in the construction of collegiate buildings opposite the church along what is now School Lane, with a separate house for the Provost or leader of the canons next to the church. The Provost's house was demolished in the early nineteenth century to be replaced by the present Wingham House, but the canons' houses, though much altered, are still standing. They are now known as The Canonry, Forge House and the Dog Inn.

Wingham's medieval expansion did not continue at the same rapid pace after the thirteenth century, as successive outbreaks of the plague slowed it down. Rather than developing into a town, it remained a village of about four hundred souls. It was prosperous, however, as the large numbers of impressive fourteenth- and fifteenth-century timber-framed houses testify.

By the sixteenth century the largely medieval church was beginning to show its age. This can be deduced from the fact that several parishioners' wills include bequests for repair. It was at this time that the north aisle was pulled down, never to be rebuilt, and the pillars on the south aisle were replaced. These are made of wood rather than stone because tradition has it that one George Ffogarde, a Canterbury brewer who was licensed to collect the money for the repair, embezzled the cash. The chestnut columns were plastered and painted to simulate stone, as shown in the Victorian print reproduced on page 24.

Development continued very slowly right up to the nineteenth century, when the population again began to increase and the village to develop. In 1801 the population stood at 844 and by 1891 had risen by over 30 per cent to 1,246. This was a direct result of the expansion of London, which created a demand for wheat, barley and market garden produce. By the time of the 1851 census the village had 230 houses, of which three were inns and seven were farms. With 78 per cent of the total acreage of Wingham owned by farmers at this time it is not surprising that the main employment was agriculture, and the dominant male occupation was that of agricultural labourer. Where industry and crafts existed these tended also to be closely related to agriculture, such as malting, milling, hurdle and harness making, and, as seen in our photographs, agricultural implement making and smithing. The mill was in use until 1912. By 1933 it had become derelict, and the tower was demolished in 1964, the remainder in the 1980s. Hop growing and drying was an important part of the local economy and continued to be so well into the twentieth century, as can be seen from the selection of photographs of the 1920s, '30s and '40s showing locals engaged in various aspects of the Wingham hop industry.

Later, the development of the East Kent coalfield gave Wingham its own railway, constructed mainly to assist in the transport of coal between Wingham and Shepherdswell. It was completed in 1912 and ran its last passenger service in 1948, although the goods traffic carried on for a few years more. In 1925 a plan had been produced by the Joint Town Planning Committee to develop Wingham as a New Town to house the increase in population that was expected to follow from the opening of eighteen new coalfields in East Kent, one of which was to be sited at Wingham. The New Town was to have 27,500 inhabitants within ten years. Steel-making was to accompany the opening up of the coalfields. It was a lucky escape for Wingham that this plan failed.

In the nineteenth century Wingham appeared able to support a large number of shops. The 1851 census lists eleven shopkeepers in the village; by 1899 this had increased to twenty-four and included shoemakers, hairdressers, tailors, ironmongers, hardware suppliers, drapers and a chemist. There were also a doctor and a vet.

Educational needs were served by Wingham School, which was founded in the nineteenth century by Sir Brook Bridges (although there had been a school in operation in 1830, according to Sir Stephen Glynne, in the south chapel of the somewhat neglected parish church). The school remained in the middle of the village in the Victorian building depicted in these photographs until after the Second World War. Then the senior boys were transferred to Sandwich and the remaining pupils moved into the old prisoner-of-war huts behind Wingham Court. These buildings continued in use until the construction of the present school in 1993.

As well as the Anglican church of St Mary the Virgin, Wingham's spiritual needs were served by a Methodist chapel and a Congregational chapel, founded in 1835 by Samuel Toomer, who was its pastor for over fifty years. However, St Mary the Virgin continued to be the main place of worship. It was extensively restored in the 1870s by Benjamin Ferry, and further restoration took place in 1923 when its bells were rehung at a cost of over £1,000. At this time the church was still divided into 200 paid and 150 free sittings.

In the inter-war period, as today, the chief landowners were the old landed aristocracy, the Fitzwalters and the Plumptres, as well as the more recently arrived Hawardens.

Despite the increased road traffic Wingham still retains much of the country charm that it possessed in the 1930s, when A.G. Bradley described his entry to the village as 'passing over a bridge which crosses a purling trout stream of clear chalk water to enter a long widish street tastefully bordered on either hand by trees'. (*England's Outpost*).

A pre-war aerial photograph of Wingham. The road to Adisham is in the bottom right-hand corner, with the High Street bisecting the right half of the picture.

Seath's Corner, showing the entrance into Wingham from the Adisham Road, 1897. Two lads stand in front of the house said to have once been 'an academy for the sons of gentlemen'.

The south end of Wingham, 1893. The house on the right in the foreground was demolished and Lloyds Bank erected when Wingham's expansion, as part of the Kent coalfield, was contemplated in 1925.

Opposite the Red Lion stands the newly built bank on the corner of Harris's Alley, 1925.

Pollarded trees in the High Street, *c.* 1910. Although acting as the photographer's props, the young boys nevertheless indicate the absence of traffic.

The Anchor Inn and the High Street, *c.* 1905. The piles of gravel on the right side of the road are for road making.

Above: Only horse traffic is to be seen in the High Street, 1816.

Left: Olive, Nellie and Ruby Joiner outside Oxenden Cottage, High Street, 1912. Joiner is an established Wingham name.

The home of the Temple family, 56 High Street, 1910. Members of the same family still lived here in 1993.

One of the oldest views of the Anchor Inn, 1907.

From the 1920s the petrol engine dominated the previous quiet of the High Street; here a charabanc party waits outside the Anchor. The cottage next door was pulled down to make way for a beer garden.

Petrol rationing during the Second World War brought some respite. This is a quiet scene from the mid-1940s.

Right: Looking up Goberry Hill from what is now St Mary's Meadow housing development, July 1950.

Below: St Mary's Meadow, 1987.

The Ship Inn. The old cottage was converted into an alehouse in 1914 and White's Brewery in nearby Stourmouth had closed by 1918, so this must be one of the earliest photographs of the inn.

The Ship Inn closed in 1975 and is now a private house.

The bridge over the river, showing the horse water-way slip, c. 1900. Beyond is the road to Sandwich and Preston.

Approximately the same scene but viewed from the opposite direction, 1983. Antique shops and restaurants have replaced some of the cottage homes.

Winter scene, 1910. Doughty's general stores is on the right.

Thatched cottages at the bottom of Preston Hill, c. 1910.

Tree felling on Preston Hill.

The Red Lion, 1900. The Sandwich to Canterbury horse-drawn coach is outside, the destination board indicating stops at Ash, Wingham and Littlebourne.

Gardner's Ash Brewery lorry supplying the Red Lion, 1935. The billboard outside advertises the Friars cinema in Canterbury, with Will Hay in *Where There's a Will There's a Way*.

The Dog Inn and the Red Lion on the Canterbury Road, possibly during the First World War. To the left of the Dog was the old forge.

Moving a short way along the Canterbury Road the next buildings are Canon Cottages, so called because in the late thirteenth century a college of canons was founded here, their homes forming an open square between this road and the old rectory. Seen outside are Mrs Gilbert and her family in around 1918.

Wingham Court and barn opposite St Mary's church, 1928.

Looking up the road from Wingham Court towards the Red Lion after the hurricane of October 1987.

St Mary's church and pond, c. 1900. The water mill was on the left-hand side of the pond. It is hard to imagine this idyllic scene when attempting to cross the road to the church today.

St Mary's church and Delbridge House, 1907. At this time the house was used as a surgery.

St Mary's church, after 1945. Parts of this building date back to AD 1200, although this has been the site of a Christian church since the Saxon period.

Above: The interior of St Mary's church. The south wall of the north aisle has been blocked but its extent can be seen on the exterior by the remains of the north aisle arch. The south aisle's stone columns were replaced in the sixteenth century by chestnut pillars from the Oxenden estate, when the finances for the restoration ran out.

Left: A Victorian print of the interior, showing the chestnut columns plastered and decorated to imitate stone.

The Festival of Harvest, 1977. From medieval times the south porch and entrance were scenes of parochial activity.

In 1990 a helicopter successfully launched the Tower Appeal. The gleaming green copper spire is a feature of the landscape for miles around.

This scene outside the west door shows the vicar, the Revd Henry Gaussen, and the Wingham bell ringers in 1923.

Archbishop Coggan, the vicar, the Revd Desmond Sampson, and members of the St Mary's church choir, 1977.

Above: The archbishop's chaplain, the vicar James Drake Brockman, the Archbishop Geoffrey Fisher and churchwardens Raymond Miles and Frank Elgar, in around 1950.

Right: The only listed churchyard wall in England with some of the parishioners, mid-1930s. Left to right: M. Pay, Mrs Hammond, Mrs McGregor (holding the infant A. Pay).

The dedication of the First World War memorial, 1920. Members of HM forces, parishioners, Scouts, Lord Fitzwalter, the vicar, the Revd Henry Gaussen, and the Congregational minister Mr Roberts were in attendance.

The procession through the village at the dedication of the war memorial.

A good study of changing dress fashion, photographed during the war memorial dedication, 1920.

Remembrance Day, c. 1932. The church parade consisted of ex-servicemen from surrounding towns and villages. After the church service members marched to the war memorial where wreaths were laid. The Revd D. Tyler, the vicar, and the congregational minister Mr Pendleton conducted the service.

The Hon. Henry Maude of Wingham Well was made the County Sheriff in 1989. Here he is seen at his installation flanked by Judge Hardcastle and the Revd Peter Brownbridge, vicar of Wingham.

The Hon. Henry Maude signing the declaration of acceptance, witnessed by Judge Hardcastle.

Right: A portrait of Samuel Elgar Toomer (1787–1870), founder member of Wingham Congregational Church in 1817 and its pastor for fifty-two years.

Below: The interior of the Congregational chapel, 1963. Since its closure it has become a home for adults with special needs, called Toomer House.

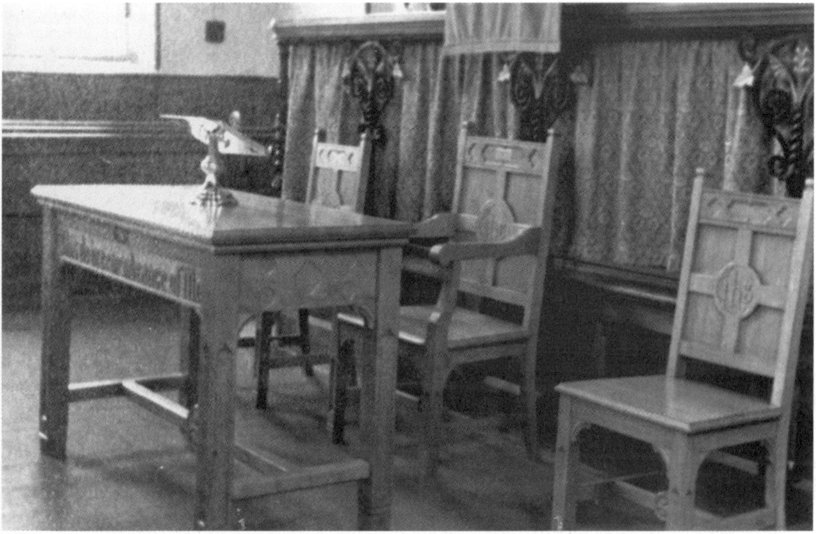

The Manse and, to the left, the Congregational chapel, 1912.

The girls' Sunday school class, June 1921. In the centre is their teacher, Mr Richardson.

A delightful group, showing the infants' Sunday school class, taken on the same day as the previous photograph. In the centre is their teacher, Mrs Gray.

Members of the congregation at the chapel fête held at The Green, Wingham Well, the home of Mr and Mrs Fagg, 1935.

The girls and infants of Wingham School in 1913; there appears to be only one boy!

These are the pupils of Wingham Girls' School, probably just after the end of the First World War.

A class of Wingham infants, with a few more boys this time, 1921.

The boys of Wingham Junior football team, 1921/2.

Wingham Girls' School, 1929. This is a more pleasing atmosphere than that shown in the infants' classroom of 1921.

The Wingham Boys' School gardening class, 1923. They are in front of the Sessions House and the constable's house with Mr Finnis.

Wingham Boys' School class, 1926. The school building was situated on the main Wingham–Sandwich road. The school was founded by Sir Brook Bridges in the nineteenth century. In 1945 the senior boys were transferred to Sandwich.

Wingham Boys' School class, 1923. Smart and smiling, these boys are a contrast with earlier photographs.

The end of the High Street, looking towards the Red Lion, 1910. In the left foreground is the butchers shop with carcases hanging outside, now a private house called Bleak Cottages.

Branford's shop on the corner by Harris's Alley, pre-1914. Mr J.J. Branford is on the cart and Mrs Anne Branford is in the doorway.

Immediately to the south of the previous scene, 1950. Here is Mr Knight the butcher, while Branford's has become Punyer's grocery shop and the electricity showroom. Mrs Rigden stands in the foreground.

The Red Lion corner, just after the end of the Second World War. The brick building to the right is the entrance to the fire station.

Another of the many changes the shop on Red Lion Corner has witnessed. In 1921 it had become Hoare's grocery shop. In the doorway is the 16-year-old Tom Rye.

High Street shops, 1926.

High Street, 1930s. The newsagent and confectionery is seen here before Mr Wiggins took it over. Its speciality was lemonade at 2d a glass.

The chemists shop. This closed in 1972, having served the community for over sixty years.

Above: Chapman's cycle shop in the High Street, 1922. Mrs Chapman and Winifred Chapman are outside.

Left: Josie and Kitty Newman outside Newman's sweetshop, 1930s. Today it is a greengrocers.

T. Judge and Son, bakers and confectioners, 1930s. Tony Sladden, Mr and Mrs Judge and Alice Hearn are standing outside. The bakery was established in 1820, and is still functioning today.

Doughty's General Stores, 1896. This shop was at the north end of the village, and is now Bridge Antiques. James Doughty, Lillian Martin and Alice Hearn are shown here.

Preston Hill sandpit, c. 1914. This was located on the right of the hill and excavated to a depth of 40 ft or more below the present level. It is possible that the sand was taken to Manston during the construction of the aerodrome.

Placing petrol tanks at Sandwich Hoy for Pratt's Petrol company, for use by Wingham Engineering plant, c. 1920.

Coppiced timber prepared for hurdle making at Waterlock, c. 1910.

Staff works photograph at Wingham Engineering, 1922. Flat caps appear to be almost universal.

Wingham Engineering Sentinel shed, 1925.

Wingham Agricultural Implement Company staff, c. 1918. They supplied all types of agricultural machinery for the local farming community.

A drawing of Wingham Agricultural Implement works, *c.* 1900.

Lovell's builders and construction works, *c.* 1900. Founded in the latter part of the nineteenth century, at one time it had over sixty employees. It was taken over later by Gregory's.

Mr Lowdell with Pat the pony, 1934. He delivered milk for Mayes dairy in Wingham, Wingham Well and Littlebourne. In June, July and August there were two deliveries daily. His wages were £2 per week, and milk cost 3d per pint.

This thatching was done at Crocksyard Farm by 'Dutch' Coleman, 1956.

Many local people were engaged in nearby Staple hop gardens, 1910. Mr Rye is wearing the trilby hat.

In the hop gardens at Wingham with the Farbrace family, 1932.

Unloading hop sacks at Twitham farm, 1920s. Mr Jack Smith of Street Farm, Wingham, is in the centre.

Dene Oasts, 1929. Dene (Dean) Farm is in the dry valley between Wingham and Adisham and was owned by the Oxendens for a long time.

Dene Oast, 1929. Dried hops were being pocketed up by Fred Rigden, Tom Bartlett and Tom Nutting.

Hop pickers at Mr Marchant's farm at Wenderton, Wingham, *c.* 1912.

Crockshard hop garden, 1930, with, left to right: Mrs Smith, Mrs Martin, Miss Hearn, Mrs Hearn, Margaret Hearn.

Picking hops for the Red Cross funds, 1940. Shown on this photograph are members of the Elgar family—Charles, Barbara, Grace, Marjorie, Ethel, Nora and Maria—with Mary Rigden and Mrs Tom Smart.

Above: Crockshard hop garden, 1930, with, left to right: Mary Pay, Mrs Deverson, Mrs Hearn (née Joiner).

Right: Left to right: Nora Temple, Rose Croucher, Winnie Davies, Mrs Chapman, 1940.

Some children in Crockshard hop garden:
Gordon, Derrick, and Daphne Pettman.

Hop stringing at Crockshard, 1948. Performing on the
stilts is 'Dutch' Coleman.

Above: Hop pickers at Crockshard, 1933, including three generations of the Bourne family. The baby in the centre is Doreen Bourne.

Right: Hop pockets ready for dispatch from Crockshard farm, with J. Hicks, 'Dutch' Coleman and Reg Coleman, 1956.

Left: Hop drying at Crockshard with J. Hicks and 'Dutch' Coleman, 1956.

Below: When hop picking had finished it was traditional for the men and women to exchange clothes. This scene was taken at Dene Farm in 1960 with, left to right, Ted Chapman, Rose Croucher, Fred Croucher, Ted Chapman jnr, Ruby Croucher and Fred Marsh.

Dried hops awaiting pressing at Pedding Farm, 1970s.

Dried hops awaiting pressing at Pedding Farm, 1970s. Mrs Constable, Mrs Moore, and Bill and Mary Rigden are present.

Pressing and bagging at Pedding, 1970s.

Testing the hop spraying machinery at Wingham, 1897.

Cutting corn at Goberry Hill during the First World War. Obviously the use of steam was still a novelty here, thus the two visitors.

Threshing at Street Farm, Wingham, 1920s. Mr Allen is on the machine, and also in the group are farmer Jack Smith and Mr Groombridge.

Left: 'Dutch' Coleman and Reg Coleman hand cutting the edges of a corn field belonging to Crockshard Farm, probably 1926.

Below: Sheep being driven along Wingham High Street, 1924.

Right: Mr Harffray's great grandfather at Hambrook (now North Court estate), *c.* 1905.

Below: Mr Deverson's cherry orchard at Wingham Green near the old railway station, 1936. Left to right: Mrs Addley, Mrs Filey, Mr Walter Marsh, Mrs N. Pettman.

Left: James and Sarah Doughty, who ran the general stores at the north end of the High Street, c. 1900.

Below: Members of the Doughty family seen a little later at a wedding celebration at Bridge Street Hall. James and Sarah Doughty are on the far right of the front row.

Right: James Aubrey Durnford aged 20, 1908. He ran Waterlock Farm, and is pictured here at Dover.

Below: Four generations of the Bourne family, 1929.

Left: The immaculately dressed Pay family, 1898. They are outside their cottage, which was situated between Preston Hill and Sandwich Hill.

Below: The wedding of Mr and Mrs Sole, 1905. They are outside the cottage shown in the photograph above.

Bill Kemsley, the church pond 'swan feeder',
c. 1890.

Mrs E. Joiner, Eileen, Mrs George Joiner and Sid
Joiner, 1922.

Mrs Pay and her daughter, later Mrs Harffrey, outside their cottage, 1902.

Constable Dale, wife and daughter posed at the gateway to the constable's house, Wingham, *c.* 1918. At PC Dale's right hand stands the cell block, and further on is the magistrate's room, later the Sessions House.

Left to right: Daphne Weston, Nurse Conway and Mrs E. Joiner at 42 High Street, 1958.

Mrs Delvere Joiner (seated) with son Frederick and his wife, 1898.

Left: Inside the home of the County High Sheriff on the day of his installation. Beside him is the banner.

Below: The Queen Mother passing along the High Street, after opening the Pilgrim's Hospice in Canterbury, 8 June 1982.

An aerial view of the Wingham section of the East Kent Light Railway, passing Wingham Engineering, after 1945.

The East Kent Light Railway line between Shepherdswell and Wingham was completed in 1912, mainly to assist in the transport of coal from the East Kent coalfields.

The East Kent Light Railway locomotive arrives at Wingham on its last passenger run. Note the steeple of St Mary's church.

The last day of the passenger service between Wingham and Shepherdswell, 3 October 1948. Mr Harffrey, stationmaster, stands with arms outstretched.

Wingham station. The modern building was purchased by the stationmaster, Mr Harffrey, for use as a garden shed at his home on the Canterbury Road when goods traffic ceased on 1 March 1951.

Wingham's first volunteer fire brigade, 1912/13. The three officers standing are Percy Branford, Charles Elgar and Ernest Lovell, with William Temple holding the horse. One of the mounted district officers was Mr Petley, who took much interest in the Wingham Brigade. He regarded it as 'the first mounted brigade in England'.

This scene was entitled 'Fire in the Square', 1920. In the centre of the picture stands Harry Bates, and to his left Mr B. Bourne.

Some of Wingham's firemen, 1921. Left to right: Freddie Coulter, Mr Bourne, James Gardner, Harry Bates, Bill Kemp.

Wingham Fire Brigade, 1932. Back row, left to right: Mr Smith (the grocer), George Tickner, Fred Coulter, Norman Bourne, Bill Bourne, Mr Gardner jnr. Middle row: Fred Tickner (the driver), Mr Kendall, Mr Bates snr, Henry Bates jnr, Mr Twiddy, Charles Butcher, -?-, -?-. Front row: Fred Elgar, Ernest Lovell, Charles Elgar.

Wingham Fire Brigade, after 1948. The station is situated between the Red Lion and the Dog. Back row, left to right: Henry Weston, Fred Tickner, Tom Nutting, Ernest Graves, Sid Joiner, Les Hogben. Front row: Norman Bourne, Claude Petley and Fred Parson.

Wingham Girls' Friendly Society holidaying at Herne Bay, 1920s. Left to right: Emmie Hulse, Phyllis Hulse, Blanche Ratcliffe, Elizabeth Philpott and Minnie Hulse.

Wingham Girls' Friendly Society at Wingham, about the same period. The back row includes Phyllis and Emmie Hulse, Lottie Morgan, Gladys Hulse. Seated are Blanche Ratcliffe, Mrs Brenchley and others.

The West Marsh Market Gardeners' outing outside the Anchor, 1920s. The fertility of the soils in this part of East Kent gave rise to many smallholdings as well as large farms.

'The Maypole Girls', 23 June 1926.

Wingham Football Club, 1925-6. Back row, left to right: Dick Groud, Norman Morris, Jim Pilcher, -?-, C. Smith, 'Bunny' Hulse. Front row: Ted Coleman, 'Tiny' Sladden, Mac Newman, Henry Weston, Fred Parsons.

Wingham Cricket Club, 1931. Back row, left to right: Mr Creswell, Frank Twiddy, W. Temple, George Lee, Jim Pilcher, F. Coughlan, Mr Vincent, Jim Graves. Front row: -?-, 'Jazz' Goodban, S. Garlinge, Norman Bourne, Mr Goodhew, Mr Chandler.

Right: Wingham Fancy Dress Show, with Derek Creed and Doreen Bourne, 1935.

Below: Wingham Football Club, 1932 3. Back row, left to right: W. Vincent, C.J. Elgar, D. Sayer, W.R. Arnold, E.R. Spice, F.E. Trowell, A.R. Medgett, E.R. Groombridge, J. Finnis. Front row: J. Davidson, F. Coughlin, W. Garlinge, E.J. Goodban, F.R. Parsons, S.H. Pay.

Wingham Girl Guide Company, early 1940s. They are at a strawberry tea at Goberry by kind invitation of Mr and Mrs Elgar.

This is thought to be a Derby Day outing, 1949.

Wingham Horticultural Society, 1934–5. The group includes Mr Pendleton (Congregational minister), Mr Coleman (postman), Mr Smith (grocer), Mr Charles Elgar and Lady Capel Cure. Where are the lady gardeners?

Wingham cricket team, 1947. Back row, left to right: V. Hulse, R. Ralph, A. Tong, A. Smart, R. Beeching, S. Bradshaw, ? Neame, J. Scott, D. Scott. Seated: R. Cork, D. Garlinge.

Wingham's Women's Institute outside the village hall, 1950s.

The Old People's WVS Christmas Tea, 1950. Among those present are Mrs Willis, Mr and Mrs Chandler, Albert Hammond, Mr Broadwood, Mrs Croucher, Mrs Maynard snr, Mrs Graves, Mrs Parsons, Nurse Gardner (local midwife), Mrs Spratt, Mrs Aston.

The British Legion cricketers, late 1940s. Back row, left to right: Jack Boakes, Fred Longley, Albert Watson, Harry Muckley, Bill Temple, Ray Tong. Front row: Mr Gardner, Jack Dimmock, Bob Salter, Bob Temple and Percy Woodward.

The Mothers' Union Nativity play, thought to be 1955.

A march past by the St John Ambulance Brigade, Wingham branch, 1957.

Officers and cadets of the St John Ambulance Brigade, 1957.

Wingham County Primary School Nativity Play, 1960. The shepherd facing the camera is Timothy Shaw. Front row, left to right: Rosemary Pagdin, Pauline Cox, Brian Jones, Kevin Finch, S. Allanson.

Signing the register: the wedding at St Mary's of Gordon Whorlow and Janet Hyde, 2 March 1968. Officiating is the Revd J. Drake Brockman.

Above: Festival of Harvest. In the background is the Old Barn, before it was demolished to make way for St Mary's Place and the road leading to St Mary's Meadow.

Left: School maypole dance at the Silver Jubilee celebrations, 1935.

The final days of the construction of Wingham Village Hall, 1936.

The opening ceremony of the Village Hall, performed by HRH the Duke of Kent, 1936.

Wingham Fire Brigade on parade at the Village Hall opening ceremony, 1936.

Celebrations to mark the coronation of King George VI and Queen Elizabeth, May 1937. This is the procession of coronation floats.

Celebrating the coronation of King George VI, May 1937. This float, created by the WI, was named 'Raggle Taggle Gypsies'.

The King and Queen coronation float, May 1937. This won first prize.

The Oriental Lanterns float, May 1937.

Wingham Fire Brigade float, May 1937. Bill Spratt is holding the horse from Crocksyard farm and Jim Beany is holding the reins. Also present are Syd Joiner, 'Darkie' Hogben and, far left, Percy Branford.

Toasting the king at Crocksyard hop garden, May 1937. Back row, left to right: Min Styering, Mrs Spratt, Mrs Kemp, Mrs Newing, Mrs Hall. Middle row: Winnie Bourne, Dolly Hogben, Mrs Croud, Mrs Spratt. Front row: Mrs Beeny, Mrs Farbrace.

The procession to mark the coronation of Queen Elizabeth II: a float is passing along the High Street, July 1953. The opportunity is being taken to advertise the flower show.

Floats in the coronation procession passing along the High Street, July 1953. Note the increased use of tractors.

A decorated tractor passing Oxenden House, July 1953.

Miss Wingham competition, 1959. Back row, left to right: Brenda Parson, Valerie Rogers, Brenda Scott, Joan Pettman, May ?, Elizabeth Hopkin, Theresa Heenan. Front row: Wendy Prebber, Miss Baker, Phyllis Hyde.

Miss Wingham with her two maids of honour on a royal progress through the High Street, 1959. Left to right: Phyllis Hyde, Wendy Prebber, Miss Baker.

Coronation of Queen of the May, 1961.

British Legion Annual Dinner, c. 1950.

Wingham Spring Fair, March 1984. This raised money for the church.

Wartime Wingham, 1941. Members of the AFS are shown here at the back of the Red Lion. Left to right: M. Bates, M.S. Linkstead, A. Harffrey, E. Pay.

Presentation of Home Guard Efficiency Cup by Major S. Miles, May 1944.

The Home Guard outside the Boys' School, 1944.

Stand-down parade of the Home Guard, having just passed the church, 26 November 1944.

Stand-down parade: the battalion on parade followed by a drumhead service, November 1944.

Wingham 700, 6 March 1986. This festival celebrated the 700th anniversary of the founding of the College of Canons by Archbishop Peckham in 1286. Queen Elizabeth I (Peggy Shaw) and lady-in-waiting (Anne Powell) are seen here.

Wingham 700: a float commemorating Lady Elizabeth de Aubrichecourt, who eloped with one of the Canons of the College.

Two

Adisham

Situated along the bottom of a chalk valley under the downs, Adisham is a small village of some seven hundred inhabitants spread over six hamlets: Cooting, Blooden, Bossington, Dane, Uffington and Adisham. For most of its existence the population has rarely risen above 400; only in the past thirty years has it almost doubled due to small housing developments along The Street and at Station Road. Its origins go back further than recorded history, probably to the pre-Roman period since pottery has been found that can be dated to the first century BC. Roman finds indicate that there may have been a settlement here after the Roman invasion in AD 54. The first permanent settlers we know of were the Jutes who, seeking a suitable site for their agrarian way of life, made their home here and gave their name to it - Aedda's Ham (homestead or village), which became Adisham in due time. The Jutes buried their dead on the top of the downs near the site of the old windmill where, in 1773, the Revd Brian Faussett excavated their remains finding remarkable jewellery and artefacts. In AD 616, only nineteen years after St Augustine converted King Ethelbert of Kent to Christianity, his son King Eadbald, in a fit of remorse for his wayward life, gave the manor of Adisham to the monks of Christ Church Priory, Canterbury, to provide their food. The home farm, or demesne, was probably bounded by the village street to the east, so the villagers' dwellings would have been situated beyond that boundary.

The oldest building remaining in Adisham is the church. This is the Norman successor to an earlier wooden structure (probably built on the site of a pagan place of worship) which would have been provided for the parish by the monks. The present building is mainly of thirteenth- and fourteenth-century construction but with evidence of the earlier cruciform church, which was probably an ecclesiastical centre for the evangelical care of the surrounding district. There was also a preaching cross, which survived until the sixteenth century. The reformation brought uncharacteristic controversy to the village when, in the Marian reversion to Catholicism, the churchwardens Richard and Valentine Austen challenged the rector John Bland's right to use the Protestant services instead of the mass. Because of his tenacious refusal to conform, Bland became one of the six Protestant martyrs burnt at the stake in Canterbury in 1558.

With the rise in poverty brought about by the Tudor economic crises, new laws in 1600-1 required the provision of a poorhouse to cater for Adisham's social casualties. It was built at Blooden and was in use until the new Union workhouse was opened at Bridge, the result of the Poor Law Amendment Act of 1834. The old poorhouse then became cottages, which were lived in until their demolition in the 1960s.

Nonconformity came early to Adisham, in the seventeenth century. Initially, when Charles Nicholls set up a dissenting congregation that did not practise infant baptism, nor come to parish services, this resulted in charges by the churchwardens since Puritan views were no longer popular after the Commonwealth of Oliver Cromwell. Anabaptists and later Baptists held meetings in their houses, and established links with the thriving chapel at Eythorne. They acquired a little thatched chapel, which was later burned down and replaced by a new brick chapel on land given by Joseph Best, a local trader. This chapel thrives still and is a centre of religious and social service to the community.

The most important house in the village was Adisham Court, the house of the bailiff who managed the monks' farm. At the dissolution of the monasteries in 1536 it passed to the Dean and Chapter of Canterbury Cathedral. During the Civil War it was occupied by Richard Dancy, a Royalist who suffered for his views when his house was plundered by soldiers who took away his horses. In a survey of 1671 he stated that the buildings were in a ruinous state, the working end of the house being propped up with timbers. For the next three centuries the land continued to be farmed by a succession of able farmers with a bevy of workers to help, in contrast to today's minimal workforce.

Education was available from the seventeenth century, a charity school being on record in the year 1700, while a dame school was said to function in the early nineteenth century and is reputed to have been housed in Dane Court. The expansion of elementary education in the mid-nineteenth century caused the Rector of Adisham, the Revd Henry Villiers, to commission a school, which was built in 1864. He and his wife, Lady Victoria, daughter of Lord John Russell, the prime minister, were enthusiastic supporters and took an active part in the life of the school—teaching, inspecting and encouraging the pupils and teachers.

The late Victorian period saw greater physical changes in Adisham's appearance as the village street filled up with sporadic building along its length; small terraces of cottages appeared and detached houses in the latest style were built for the more prosperous villagers. Local government replaced parish government in 1894 and new amenities came, such as a village hall in 1905 and the church room in 1909. Here villagers formed an institute to engage in practical communal activities such as handicrafts and harvest suppers. Agriculture was the principal employer at this time: small farms and ancillary crafts associated with them, such as the blacksmith, carpenter, wheelwright, shoemaker, and jobs in the hop industry, provided the necessities of life and gave employment. The coming of the London, Chatham and Dover Railway increased employment and provided easier travel when it was opened in 1861, rendering horse-drawn carriers' vans almost obsolete. Their final demise came in the 1930s with the arrival of the motor van and the bus. Local authority housing provided improved living conditions for villagers who had been housed previously in ancient cottages without basic sanitation. The houses at West View and Station Road were built in the '30s, and after the Second World War more council houses were provided. Old cottages like the forge and Oast Cottages near the school were demolished and private building development took place along The Street, linking the sporadic developments of the late nineteenth and early twentieth centuries. As more people acquired cars so the village shops disappeared—the butcher, baker and the second grocer closed down when people began to patronize the new supermarkets. Today Adisham has just one general store with its post office, which was started so successfully by Fred Best in the mid-nineteenth century. A new village hall has replaced the church room and the old village hall, while thriving new groups such as the playgroup, WI and keep fit classes continue the tradition of participation in community life.

Right: Church Hill before road widening, 1962.

Below: Holy Innocents church and pond, c. 1918. The church was once probably a minster and centre for priests ministering to the surrounding settlements. The pond in the foreground—the largest in Kent—was filled in 1962 when the road was straightened. The car belonged to Dr MacElwain. The house beside the pond, known as Elm House, once included a shop kept by Rebecca Joiner.

Adisham Church.

Hoskins's Photo Series

Adisham pond, looking north, c. 1929. Cricket was played in the field to the top left of the picture. Also shown is the cricket hut beside the dyke from which water was drawn for its copper boiler.

Adisham Pond, c. 1930. In 1933 Kent historian Charles Igglesden told how many a driver on a dark night found himself and his horse and cart straying into the waters. Reference to the pond occurs as early as 1283.

A view of the Bull Inn and Pond Cottages, c. 1930. The house at the start of Church Lane opposite the Bull Inn was called Hammel Cottage. It was positioned at right angles to the street, its door facing towards the pond. It was lived in by a Mrs Garlinge in 1920, but has now been demolished.

The Street, looking south from the Bull Inn, showing the New Farm Cottages built around 1914. No. 1 was first lived in by the Payne family. Until 1929 the Saffreys lived at no. 2 and were followed by the Garlinge family. At no. 3 lived the Fielder family, whose father was the village policeman. At no. 4 lived the Hedges family.

The Street, looking north, *c.* 1931. On the left is the old church room, demolished in 1977 when the new village hall was built. The area of open land between the village hall and New Farm Cottages, which today is filled with housing, was formerly the bowling alley—according to the tithe award map of 1821.

Looking across The Street from the field opposite the school, *c.* 1962. The large block of dwellings in the middle ground is the eighteenth-century malthouse known as Oast Cottages, demolished to make way for Mummery Place flats. The building under repair next to the school was the wash-house used by the residents of the cottages.

The original village hall, built in 1905 beside Oast Cottages. It was used as the Village Institute, where men of the village carried out social activities. During the Second World War it was used by the Home Guard and as a first aid post.

The Street, looking north, c. 1920. On the left is Whitehall, now known as Plum Tree Cottage, a smallholding and a brick-built house with a timber framework inside that dates back to the seventeenth century, when it was probably occupied by Thomas and Vincent Ladd, who were prominent dissenters. Beyond Whitehall is the bakery and home of Joseph Best, the baker. Among the people in the picture are May Pearce (in centre) and to the left of the group John Garlinge.

The Street, *c.* 1920. This remains virtually unaltered today. The cottages (Black Row) in the right foreground, known as the Tarpots, were built for the workers constructing the railway in the 1860s, and were demolished in the early 1960s. Behind the Tarpots, Chapel Cottages, which are still standing, were built in 1886. Note the gas street lighting in the foreground. The children in the picture are, on the left, Bernard Gill, the headmaster's son, and on the right Lesley Bough, who lived at Hillside Cottages. On the left of the picture are Chapel Villas.

Woodlands Corner, *c.* 1926. On the left is the lane to the 'Ale House', a somewhat ramshackle lean-to construction used by local drinkers. To the right, behind the horse, can be seen the thatched cottage belonging to the Newingtons, since demolished. The large coniferous tree on the right was cut down in 1962. Shown with the large carthorse is Frank Piddock, who was 17 at the time and lived at Dane Court. Of the people in the distance, the man to the right is George Prebble, a farm worker.

A view of the hamlet of Blooden, c. 1928. It was renamed Upper Adisham in the nineteenth century. The hamlet's origins can be traced back to Saxon times. The houses in the left foreground still stand, though the thatched cottages have been demolished. The old building on the right hand side was the former village poorhouse, later renamed Blooden Cottages and demolished in 1960. Shown in the picture are Mrs Spain and her daughter Margaret, who lived at Blooden Cottages.

Adisham Court, c. 1930. The medieval house was replaced by a later house in the seventeenth century with typical Dutch-style gable, indicative of Flemish influence. The present house was completely gutted and rebuilt in the 1930s. This photo was probably taken soon after its rebuilding.

Manor Farm, *c. 1930*. The exterior dates from the first half of the eighteenth century. In 1731, through the marriage of Thomas Reynolds to the heiress Elizabeth Pilcher, the property passed to the Reynolds family, with whom it remained until the 1890s. In 1934 a Mr R.S. Poile lived here. It remained a working farm until the 1960s, but is now a private house.

Manor Farm in its working days. This farm, the back part of which dates back to the early sixteenth century, was probably the home of one of the Austen brothers who were responsible for indicting John Bland, the Adisham martyr. In the eighteenth century it was the home of William Reynolds, brother of John, the pioneer farmer of Dane Court (see p. 109). The ancient barn belonging to this farm was destroyed by fire in 1965.

Court Lodge, c. 1930. This house also dates from the seventeenth century. In the background can be seen the new war memorial.

Hazelmere, built at the beginning of the twentieth century, early 1930s. Standing by the garden roller is Mr Gill, the schoolmaster. He encouraged the boys of the school to cultivate the field next to his house.

Edelweiss, also built at the beginning of the twentieth century, pictured in the early 1930s, when it was the home of Mr F. Best. He was responsible for publishing many of the photos used in this book, and sold them in his grocers shop next door.

Myrtle Villa. This house, built at the turn of the century, was lived in by Mr Henry Hold in 1918. Later it was the home of Miss Agnes Best.

Ivy Cottage, left, and Vine Cottage, right. In 1723 Elizabeth Reynolds married Sam Spratt of Wingham and as a wedding gift or dowry her father, Thomas Reynolds, either built or completely reconstructed Ivy Cottage. Vine Cottage was demolished in 1926.

Dane Court, 1963. The house was built in around 1430, probably by Thomas Denne of Barham. By the end of the seventeenth century it had passed into the hands of the Reynolds family, who farmed there for over two centuries. The best known member of the family was John Reynolds (1706-79). He won local and national acclaim for his innovative farming methods, notably the introduction of the Swedish turnip for animal fodder for winter feeding. The house began as a three-bay timber-framed hall house, ceiled over in the sixteenth century and encased in brick at the beginning of the seventeenth century. By the middle of the nineteenth century there were at least two families living there, the house having become two farm cottages for Woodlands Farm.

Holmleigh, built at the beginning of the twentieth century. It was lived in by the local coal merchant, James Pegden, who also acted as a carrier in the early 1920s.

The Woodlands, Adisham.

Woodlands, 1920s. Situated above the village in an attractive parkland setting, this house was built by John Dilnott in the early nineteenth century. He was the father-in-law of Rachel Reynolds, granddaughter of John Reynolds of Dane Court.

Great Cooting Farm House, c. 1900. All traces of the original house, first mentioned as a holding in 1187, have been lost. Its foundations may be in the paddock adjoining. The rear portion of the house is the oldest, with timbers and a bread oven constructed in the late seventeenth century. The front was built during the 1850s. In 1938 a dene hole, or vertical chalk pit with chamber, was unearthed nearby.

Great Cooting, Adisham.

In the 1930s Great Cooting was still attached to a working farm, in the hands of Ernest Mummery, who is still living in the village today.

Bossington House. The sixteenth-century part of this house was the original rectory of Adisham and remained so until the early twentieth century, when a new one was constructed nearer the church. In the mid-nineteenth century it was considerably enlarged, probably during the tenure of the Villiers family, since their ten children and numerous servants would have required more room. In July 1984 a trench was cut for new water mains and human bones were discovered. Archaeologists located a further series of burials, possibly of plague victims.

The Street, c. 1900. Shopkeepers are outside their premises. Also in the picture is a cart, which may have been the village carrier's. To the left is the post office, grocery and general store of Fred Best, with the butchers next door. Opposite is the bakers, run by Joseph Best.

The earliest known photo of the post office and general stores, *c.* 1890. This was before the refronting of the shop. The shop windows have a mid-nineteenth century appearance and the right hand side appears to be an earlier building. The left hand side has its store room doors, while the bay windows of the first floor have yet to be fitted. Beside the shop is Bank House, in which Henry Champ the boot repairer lived.

The shop, *c.* 1900. The butcher, probably William Lawrence, is standing outside his shop on the right. The frontage has changed with the addition of bay windows in the bedrooms and shop fronts.

Above: The Street, *c.* 1930. Very little has changed except for the cars parked outside the grocers. The bakers and the bakery are both now private houses.

Left: The post office, possibly at the time of the coronation of King George VI.

The bakers shop, *c.* 1910. The baker's delivery cart toured the village and surrounding area. To the left is Whitehall.

The baker's delivery cart, *c.* 1930.

Adisham Smock Mill, c. 1909. A mill was mentioned in records in the fourteenth century, when it belonged to the monks of Christ Church, Canterbury. It was still in use in 1905.

After it had been struck by lightning in 1892 the mill was repaired at a cost of £42. By 1932 it was reported as being in a derelict state and no longer in use. In 1933 it burnt down.

The Mill House, *c.* 1909. Standing at the highest point of Adisham Downs just inside the old parish boundary, this was the home and the business premises of the miller. Today it is a private house.

Adisham station, *c.* 1910. The London, Chatham and Dover Railway from Canterbury to Dover was completed in 1861. The stationmaster's house and the old ticket office with its ladies' waiting room can be seen.

Adisham station goods yard. A thriving coal yard operated from here, distributing coal from the Snowdown colliery. There was no station at Aylesham at this time.

Outside Eidelweiss, c. 1930.

The Bull, c. 1920. This public house dates back at least to the sixteenth century. In 1932 it was recorded that the building had recently been renovated. The original sixteenth-century building stood at right angles to the road. The off-sales counter was in the door on the right hand side of the photo.

Forge Cottage next to Woodlands Farm. The cottage and its forge are recorded in the seventeenth century. These buildings were demolished in 1962 and bungalows were built on the site.

Above: The water tower, 1903. Workers and their families pose beside the nearly completed tower. They appear to have been celebrating a wedding, and the baby has a splendid carriage.

Left: The water tower, 1903.

Adisham School, 1900. This was built in 1864 as a result of the enthusiasm of Lady Victoria Villiers, wife of the rector, Henry Villiers, who was son of the Bishop of Durham. To help fund the building she sold jewellery that had been given her as a wedding gift by Parliament, her father being Lord John Russell, the prime minister. The builder was Mr William Crothall, whom the Villiers consulted frequently during the school's construction. There were two classrooms, one for boys and one for girls.

Adisham School, 1898. The master is Mr George Streeting who took over in 1895. The girl in front of Mr Streeting is Agnes Best, who in 1910 saw Blériot fly over Dover (see p. 129).

Adisham School, 1900. The headmaster is still Mr Streeting. The children are dressed in their Sunday best, many sporting flowers as buttonholes. The mothers are just visible behind the hedge. Agnes Best is in the third row up, fifth from the left.

Adisham School, 1903.

Adisham School, 1920. The headmaster, Mr Gill, was appointed in 1909; notice he is still wearing puttees, presumably a legacy from wartime service. Top row, left to right: J. Crick, J. Wilson, H. Garlinge, ? Newington, B. Penfold, A. Medgett, S. Bicker, C. Oxtoby, G. Stewart.

Adisham School, 1922. Among the front row are M. Garlinge, F. Simmonds, P. Fielder, B. Pegden, I. Penfold, G. Bicker.

Above: Gardening class, 1919. Boys under the supervision of Mr Gill and the gardening instructor work in the field opposite the school, which is unchanged to this day. Among the group are C. Oxtoby, R. Penfold, G. Stewart, A. Medgett, A. Garlinge, S. Stannard, A. Crick, S. Bicker, J. Crick, G. Stannard (still living in the village), H. Garlinge, G. Wilson.

Left: Gardening instructor, 1920.

Adisham Village Men's Institute, 1921. Outside the original village hall, it fostered handicraft among village men and was encouraged by the rector, the Revd Harry Cartwright. In the front row are Mr True, F. Best (proprietor of the post office and stores), A. Atkins, J. Best (the baker). Others are Mr Baker, Mr Gill, Mr Sampson, H. Champ (shoemaker), Mr Arnold, Mr Impett, C.B. Hoskings, Mr Dowle, T. Friend, A. Simmonds.

Holy Innocents church, 1921. The church now standing dates from the thirteenth century but contains some eleventh-century material. In 1869 it was completely restored by Henry Villiers. The roof was altered and the battlements on the tower were replaced by the present pointed roof.

Church interior, c. 1900. Note the oil lamps.

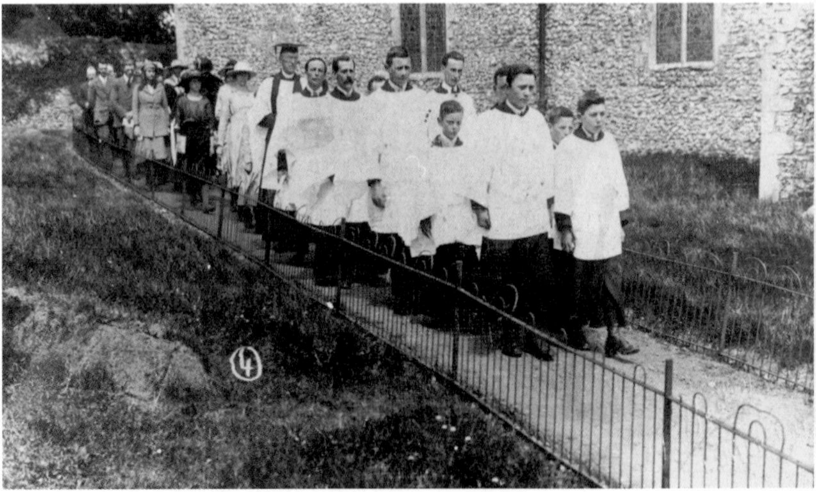

The church choir, 1921. The rector is the Revd Harry Cartwright.

Dedication of the war memorial in the new graveyard, 1921. The memorial was made by J.H. Wilson of Adisham (left of memorial); Bateman of Canterbury made the inscription. The last post was played by two soldiers from Canterbury barracks. Mrs Fox (centre of photo) lost a son, Alfred, aged eighteen.

Dedication of the war memorial. Fred Best can be seen next to the cross.

Opening the memorial gates, 1921. These were placed at the entrance to the recreation ground, which had been donated to the village by the Church Commissioners to commemorate the signing of the Peace Treaty in 1919. They were made by Gordon Medgett. The opening was performed by Lord Hawarden of Bossington House, who was involved in many of the social organisations in the village.

The pipe band on parade at the dedication of the gates, 1921. To the left of the picture are George Stannard and his father.

.... 19 . 12 1910

My Dear Mother –

Very pleased to have your letter this morning & to have such good news from Bank House. The flying man went over here but of course I did not see it. I am having a very nice time here have taken Baby out this afternoon he is a dear little mite. Auntie says she would like a 3/- best cake & a 2/- seed one for Xmas please. Went to Baker this morning & am to go again tomorrow at 10.30 cannot say yet when I shall return. Had a P.C from Aunt Peg this morning giving me a little pluck. Mr Morrow at Chapel yesterday was very nice. With love to all. Aggie

Above: Miss Agnes Best's postcard, 1910. This was written by Agnes to her mother, wife of Adisham's baker Mr Joseph Best, recording the sighting of Blériot in the first aeroplane to cross the Channel. Miss Best ended her days at Myrtle Villa, Adisham.

Right: Mr Birch of Blooden with his handmade tapestry, which he probably made at the Village Institute.

129

Servants at Bossington House, 1930s. Left to right: -?-, Miss Philpott (parlour maid), Jean Scothorn (Mrs Alfred Medgett), Eugenie (housemaid).

Old People's Supper, 1924. The Hon. Mrs James with the oldest lady, Mrs Hannah Atkins, and the oldest man, Mr Claringbould (aged 88), with Mr Fred Best in the background.

Right: The Best family, 1900.

Below: Adisham viaduct, 1928/9. Left to right: Frances Fielder, Edith Horner, Marjorie Horner (in front), Joyce Horner. The dog is Rover. The pile of chippings was kept at the corner of the field to repair the road. This area was known as Monk's Hole, probably a corruption of Monk's Sole (Pond).

Gardeners' outing, 1958. Among the group are Mr Medgett (Adisham's last wheelwright and coffin maker), Miss Beryl Pegden, Mrs Dowle, Miss Aggie Best, Mrs Medgett, Mrs Doris Best, Mr Joe Best, Mrs Lutman, Mrs Petts, Mr Alf Fry, Mrs Fry, Mrs Marsh, Pat Baker and Mrs Postin.

Group outing, 1966. In the photo are, among others, Mr Ernest Mummery, Mr Claude Hosking, Mr G. Medgett, Mr J. Best, Mrs Best, Mrs Mummery, Mr Hampshire (the bus driver), Mrs Mummery, Miss Aggie Best, Mrs Medgett, Mrs Postin, Mrs Marsh, Mrs Pout, Mrs Orchard and Mrs Lutman.

Outing to Kew, 1966. This was arranged by Mr Peter Davies (back row, second left), and others are Martin Woodward, Alfred Fry, Mrs 'Dot' Simpson (front row, centre), in charge of the village shop for many years. Also in the front row are Mrs Nancy Beer, Mrs Peter Davies, Jeanette Simpson and Mrs Hall. In the middle row are Norman Pout, Mrs Fry and Mr Shaw. At the back are Alf Fry, Mrs Orchard, Mr Orchard and Mr Gambrell, who kept the post office.

Beating the bounds, 1968. This party set off to beat the bounds of the village, using several village boys to be 'impressed' by the beating and the boundary stones! Jack Watts, Chairman of the Parish Council and a Special Constable of long standing, who lived at Whitehall, leads the way. Beside him is Terry Burke, accompanied by one of the boundary boys, Mark Crane. Following them are Mrs Burke and Mr Hobbs.

Above: Wartime Adisham. This railway gun, manned by the Royal Artillery 2nd Super Heavy 16th Battery, defended 'Bomb Alley', as this part of Kent was known.

Left: A wartime romance preceded the wedding of Jim and Freda Woodward, 15 August 1945. The bride carried red, white and blue flowers and the National Anthem was sung.

Three

Littlebourne

Littlebourne is the farthest downstream of the three Bourne villages, the others being Bishopsbourne and Bekesbourne. These are the ones affected by the intermittent stream, or Nail Bourne, which flows when the water table is sufficiently high.

As with much of the land in the Little Stour valley, Littlebourne belonged to the Church, but unlike Ickham and Wickhambreux it was a poor benefice, having only the Vicarage with the small tithes for its incumbent, while the Rectory with its great tithes was let for centuries to a lay tenant, and was finally sold in 1864. The Church Commissioners kept Littlebourne Court until 1922, when it was sold to the Mount family and the change to fruit farming began. Its proximity to Canterbury and its position on the main road to Sandwich accelerated change in other ways. It has suffered more losses of its old buildings and gardens to make way for modern development, and the heavy traffic through the main street is a problem.

One of its most attractive features is the river. The Little Stour flows along the edge of the village towards Wickhambreux. Its course was altered to accommodate two watermills, one belonging to Ickham parish. Besides the Nail Bourne, the springs at Well Chapel and all down the valley add to its flow.

The mill nearest to Littlebourne was in fact Ickham Mill. It was burnt down in about 1908. There was a medieval watermill on this site and a waterway called The Gryke.

Littlebourne Mill is halfway to Wickhambreux and was part of Littlebourne Manor. It was still working under water power until 1944, when it was electrified by Hovis, who put a large sign on the side, and it became known as the Hovis Mill. It has now been converted into a house.

There is a church at Littlebourne mentioned in the Domesday Book, but the present one was built in the thirteenth century by the monks of St Augustine's Abbey. They owned the manor and rectory at that time. Later they gave the Rectory to the Pope as a bribe, and had to provide a vicarage.

The Rectory was built at the beginning of the seventeenth century or earlier, but this oldest part was demolished when the bungalow estate was built on the rectory garden. The present Rectory is eighteenth century with later additions. The Vicarage is further towards Wickhambreux and is in two parts, the front early seventeenth century with a Flemish gable and porch, and the Victorian wing behind.

The United Reformed chapel was originally next to the Vicarage, built there in about 1830 when John Davis owned the land. In 1881 the land was sold to Margaret Wray, who built The Villa. She was the vicar's wife's sister. The chapel was then taken down brick by brick and re-erected on its present site.

Meadow View in Nargate Close was the original school, built in 1844 by Charles James, lessee of the Rectory. It was always connected with the Church and moved to a new building in 1871. This is now called the Old School. When first built it had a bell tower and ventilation holes (which leaked). The new school opposite the church was opened in 1971.

Up until the Second World War, Littlebourne, like other villages, was self sufficient. It had two butchers, four grocers, a hardware/haberdashery/clothing stores, a post office and newsagent, as well as a saddler, laddermaker, shoe menders, plumbers, builder and decorator, forge and blacksmith. There were several malthouses, hop kilns and breweries as well as four public houses, one of which is now a house.

Entertainments were also village based: fêtes and flower shows, penny readings, magic lantern shows, Christmas and Easter concerts in the church and chapel, and Mrs Hutson's Band in The Hut (the predecessor of the Village Hall). There were also other clubs: Rifle, Cricket, Football, and Rat and Sparrow, for vermin extermination. For those preferring quieter pursuits there was a library in a house called Carib organized by Mrs Cobbold, and the Girls' Friendly Society had a choir and taught needlework and embroidery. The boys still found time to take around the Guy, play tricks with peoples' door knockers and use their catapults.

There is still plenty to do and join, though most people work elsewhere, but these photographs help recreate the village as it used to be.

The old bridge and the ford over the Little Stour early in the twentieth century.

The river, and the garden of Littlebourne House.

Tom Wood, the river keeper.

Ickham Mill, which was burnt down in around 1908.

Littlebourne Mill, which is now a house, showing the sign that gave it the name the Hovis Mill.

A view of the High Street, showing Ryes newsagent in the foreground on the right and the old malthouse on the left.

High Street, showing Hollaway's general store on the left, and to its right the post office.

Staff and soldiers outside Hollaway's hardware store in Nargate Street, c. 1914.

Right: Mr Best, Mr Hollaway's uncle, who used to deliver groceries in the 1930s.

Below: Reynolds, one of Littlebourne's two butchers shops.

Newports, Littlebourne's other butchers shop.

Mr Johnstone's shop in Bekesbourne Lane, 1960s.

Mr Jackson's tobacconist shop in the High Street, 1960s.

The Anchor Inn.

The Square, showing the Anchor on the left and in the foreground on the right the King William (formerly known as the King's Head), c. 1905. The horse and cart are drawn up in front of the oast houses.

A view of the King William, with Littlebourne House to its right, c. 1890.

The Evenhill decorated for the Jubilee of King George V and Queen Mary, 1935.

Church Road, showing the old Basketmakers pub (foreground) and the new Basketmakers (rear), c. 1910.

Satisfied customers outside the Basketmakers, 1914–18.

The Basketmakers between the wars.

Old Brewery House, Nargate Street, where the brewer lived.

The brewery and malthouse, Nargate Street, one of several in the village.

The old malthouse, malthouse cottages and the charity cottages, 1960s.

Maltsters and waggoners outside the malthouse. To the right can be seen the old harness shop.

Mr Huston, the village saddler and harness maker.

The oast house and cottages at Evenhill.

115945 The Oast, Littlebourne

The old oast house and, to its left, the Poor House, Evenhill, 1930s.

'Hopping' at Garrington between the wars. The man standing top left is Tubby Cornwall.

A stack of 5-bushel baskets for hop picking, made by C. Rolfe and Son, Littlebourne basket makers, 1908.

One of Littlebourne's first cars, 1920s.

Village children like Gwen Williams cycled to school in Canterbury during the 1920s.

Local tradesman in the High Street, between the wars.

High Road, Littlebourne.

Holloway's Photo Series.

Above: Looking towards Leigh Priory, three modes of transport are visible: walking, cycling and driving.

Right: St Vincent's church, Littlebourne, before the addition of the porch.

A view of the church, c. 1900.

The east end of the church with the tithe barn behind.

The seventeenth-century Old Vicarage in Nargate Street, showing its Dutch gabling and the Victorian additions.

Elmleigh, Littlebourne.

G.N. Hollaway, Littlebourne P.O.

The Old Rectory, which dates from the eighteenth century but has later additions.

Cricket on the village green early in the twentieth century.

The Manor House and oasts.

The High Street, between the wars.

The village fête was held in the grounds of the Old Rectory in Edwardian times.

Littlebourne Guides.

The Girls' Friendly Society, 1900s.

The village cricket team between the wars.

A view of Albion House School, a private school in Poplar Street early in the twentieth century.

Acknowledgements

Special thanks are due to Gilda Sumner and Ann Powell of Wingham History Society who worked with Maurice Crane to put together the Wingham section of this book. Without their special knowledge of the village and familiarity with the photographs this book would not have been possible. Wingham History Society would like to thank all those who have contributed in any way to the photographic collection, for sharing the personal memories which helped to identify people and places, and who generously gave permission for their inclusion in this book. Thanks are also due to Messrs John Smith, Harry Turner and Mike Waterman for the photographic work they did that helped to make the production possible.

Thanks are also due to the people of Adisham, especially the Best and Woodward families, who loaned photographs, to Harry Amson who reproduced many of them and to Joyce Payne, whose remarkable memory provided many of the personal memories of Adisham's past.

Finally, I would like to thank Elizabeth Jefferies, who so generously agreed to compile the Littlebourne section of the book.

J.A.C.